20 FUN FACTS ABOUT THE RESPIRATORY SYSTEM

T0022649

BY ZELDA SALT

Gareth Stevens
PUBLISHING

Please visit our website, www.garethstevens.com. For a free color catalog of all our high-quality books, call toll free 1-800-542-2595 or fax 1-877-542-2596.

Library of Congress Cataloging-in-Publication Data

Names: Salt, Zelda, author.
Title: 20 fun facts about the respiratory system / Zelda Salt.
Description: New York : Gareth Stevens Publishing, [2019] | Series: Fun fact file: body systems | Includes index.
Identifiers: LCCN 2018031030| ISBN 9781538229255 (library bound) | ISBN 9781538232804 (pbk.) | ISBN 9781538232811 (6 pack)
Subjects: LCSH: Respiratory organs–Juvenile literature. | Respiration–Juvenile literature.
Classification: LCC QP121 .S15 2019 | DDC 612.2–dc23
LC record available at https://lccn.loc.gov/2018031030

First Edition

Published in 2019 by
Gareth Stevens Publishing
111 East 14th Street, Suite 349
New York, NY 10003

Copyright © 2019 Gareth Stevens Publishing

Designer: Sarah Liddell
Editor: Meta Manchester

Photo credits: Cover, p. 1 (main) Life science/Shutterstock.com; file folder used throughout David Smart/Shutterstock.com; binder clip used throughout luckyraccoon/Shutterstock.com; wood grain background used throughout ARENA Creative/Shutterstock.com; p. 5 Patrick Foto/Shutterstock.com; p. 6 Charles Daghlian/Patho/Shutterstock.com; p. 7 Alexander_ Safonov/Shutterstock.com; p. 8 MCarper/Shutterstock.com; p. 9 Lopolo/Shutterstock.com; p. 10 adriaticfoto/Shutterstock.com; pp. 11, 23 Sebastian Kaulitzki/Shutterstock.com; p. 12 VectorMine/Shutterstock.com; p. 13 FGC/Shutterstock.com; pp. 14, 21 Nerthuz/ Shutterstock.com; p. 15 neneo/Shutterstock.com; p. 16 Sergey Novikov/Shutterstock.com; p. 17 Lightspring/Shutterstock.com; p. 18 Pavel Chagochkin/Shutterstock.com; pp. 19, 27 (inset) crystal light/Shutterstock.com; p. 20 Domenic Gareri/Shutterstock.com; p. 22 Littlekidmoment/Shutterstock.com; p. 24 Olesia Bilkei/Shutterstock.com; p. 25 wavebreakmedia/Shutterstock.com; p. 26 AFP Contributor/Contributor/AFP/Getty Images; p. 27 (main) Alila Medical Media/Shutterstock.com; p. 29 MANDY GODBEHEAR/ Shutterstock.com.

Printed in the United States of America

CPSIA compliance information: Batch #CW19GS: For further information contact Gareth Stevens, New York, New York at 1-800-542-2595.

CONTENTS

Words in the glossary appear in **bold** type the first time they are used in the text.

BREATHE IN, BREATHE OUT

On average, you take between 17,280 and 23,040 breaths a day! You mostly don't notice thanks to special cells in the brain that control breathing. Lots of things can change how you breathe, including how you feel and how much you move around.

Breathe in and out a few times right now. You took in a gas called oxygen and let out the gas carbon dioxide. Your amazing respiratory system did that! If it were to stop for even a few minutes, you'd be in big trouble!

You use your respiratory system all the time without even thinking about it!

A THIRD OF THE OXYGEN YOU BREATHE IN IS USELESS.

This oxygen doesn't do anything. It's called "dead air" because it never makes it into your bloodstream. The rest of the oxygen you inhale, or breathe in, is carried by red blood cells to the heart so it can be pumped to the rest of your body.

When you inhale through your mouth and nose, air moves down your trachea, or windpipe. It's lined with **mucus** and tiny hairlike structures called cilia that keep dust and other harmful **particles** from entering your lungs.

You can see the water in your breath when you exhale onto glass.

YOU DON'T JUST BREATHE OUT AIR — YOU ALSO BREATHE OUT WATER!

About 0.59 fluid ounces (17.4 ml) while resting, to be exact. This is because the inside of your body is very warm, which makes the air you exhale, or breathe out, **humid**. You breathe out even more water when you exercise!

FUN FACT: 3

HAIR IN YOUR NOSE PROTECTS YOUR LUNGS!

Nose hair **filters** the air you breathe as it enters the body. It helps stop dust, pollen, and other harmful particles from entering your lungs.

Don't pluck! Your nose hairs are an important way your body keeps you from breathing in anything harmful.

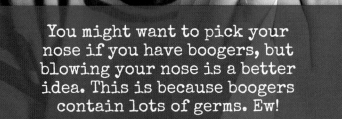

You might want to pick your nose if you have boogers, but blowing your nose is a better idea. This is because boogers contain lots of germs. Ew!

MUCUS PROTECTS YOUR RESPIRATORY SYSTEM.

The mucus in your nose traps dust, dirt, and other particles. This creates boogers! Mucus also keeps the inside of your nose moist and warms up the air you breathe.

Sneezing is one of the ways your body gets rid of germs. Cover your mouth when you feel a sneeze coming on!

FUN FACT: 5

YOUR SNEEZES CAN TRAVEL AS FAST AS A CAR.

Some scientists believe the air let go when you sneeze might reach speeds of around 100 miles (161 km) per hour! Others think the actual speed is much lower, but sneeze goo can still travel up to 26 feet (8 m) away!

LARYNX LOWDOWN

YOUR LUNGS HELP YOU TALK!

When you talk, you're actually exhaling. That's why you have to stop speaking to inhale again. As you exhale, air passes from your lungs, through your trachea and larynx, and hits your vocal cords. Sound is made when air flows between your closed vocal cords.

The larynx is sometimes called the voice box. Your vocal cords lay across the larynx.

11

YOU CAN BLAME YOUR EPIGLOTTIS IF YOU CHOKE!

The epiglottis is a special flap at the top of the larynx. It opens so air can enter the trachea. It closes when you swallow so food and drink don't "go down the wrong tube." If your epiglottis doesn't close fast enough, you could choke!

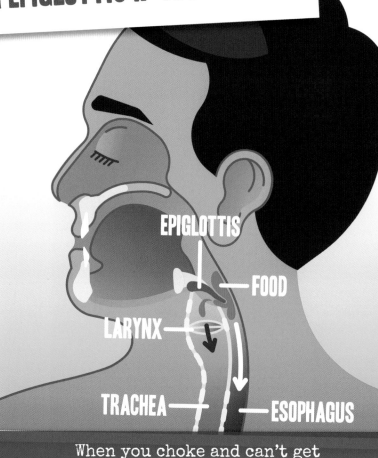

EPIGLOTTIS

FOOD

LARYNX

TRACHEA

ESOPHAGUS

When you choke and can't get enough air to breathe, your body makes you cough to try to push the stuck object back up into your throat.

ARE THEY CHOKING?

LIPS AND SKIN TURNING
BLUE OR GRAYISH

PASSING OUT

NOISY OR SQUEAKY
BREATHING SOUNDS

CAN'T TALK

SKIN LOOKING RED,
THEN TURNING BLUISH

TROUBLE BREATHING

WEAK COUGH

These are common signs that someone
is choking. If you think someone is
choking, let an adult know right away
and call 911. If you're choking, you
can let other people know by holding
your neck with one or both hands.

13

LOVELY LUNGS

YOU HAVE TWO LUNGS, BUT THEY DON'T LOOK THE SAME!

The right lung is a little shorter and wider than the left lung. This is because the left lung shares space with your heart, and the right lung shares space with your liver.

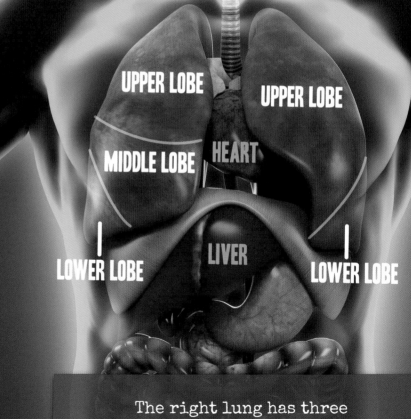

UPPER LOBE

UPPER LOBE

MIDDLE LOBE

HEART

LOWER LOBE

LIVER

LOWER LOBE

The right lung has three parts, called lobes. The left lung only has two lobes.

Pope Francis has only one lung! The other was removed when he was a teenager because of a bad illness.

YOU CAN LIVE WITH ONLY ONE LUNG!

If one lung is removed, the remaining lung grows bigger to make up the difference. You won't be able to breathe quite as well, but you can still have a pretty normal life. People with a single lung have even run **marathons**!

15

FUN FACT: 10

EXERCISE MAKES YOUR LUNGS BETTER AT THEIR JOB.

Exercise—such as playing sports, going for a run, or dancing—keeps you healthy. Besides making your **muscles** stronger, it also improves how your lungs take in oxygen and share it with other parts of your body.

THE LUNGS HAVE A "TREE" INSIDE THEM.

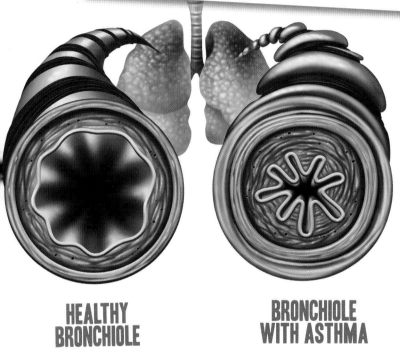

HEALTHY BRONCHIOLE

BRONCHIOLE WITH ASTHMA

Asthma is an illness that makes it hard for someone to breathe. In someone with asthma, the walls of the bronchioles contract, or get smaller, which makes it harder for air to pass through.

The bronchial tree starts where the trachea splits into two bronchi branches, one in each lung. The bronchi then split into smaller branches called bronchioles, which also split into even smaller parts called alveoli.

17

HEALTHY
LUNGS

Healthy lungs are the only **organ** that will float on water. Lungs that are sick will sink.

SICK LUNGS

YOUR LUNGS COULD FLOAT ON WATER.

Even after you breathe out all the way out, there's always some air left in your lungs. Lungs also have millions of balloon-like structures called alveoli. Alveoli are tiny air sacs found at the end of the bronchioles.

ON AVERAGE, ADULTS HAVE ABOUT 480 MILLION ALVEOLI.

ALVEOLI

Alveoli are filled with tiny blood **vessels** called capillaries. This is where carbon dioxide in blood is exchanged for oxygen. Oxygen-rich blood then travels to cells throughout the rest of the body.

A tennis court is 2,808 square feet (261 sq m)—even half of that is a lot of lung!

YOUR LUNGS, FLATTENED OUT, MIGHT COVER HALF A TENNIS COURT!

There are many tiny parts inside your lungs. Scientists have tried to figure out their total **surface area**. Some think the surface area might be larger than half a tennis court, but it's hard to get an exact measurement.

MIGHTY MUSCLES

AIR ISN'T WHAT MAKES YOUR CHEST MOVE WHEN YOU BREATHE.

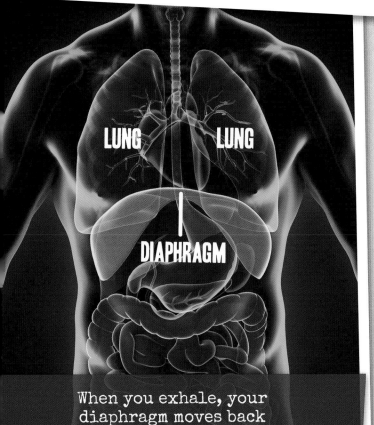

LUNG LUNG

DIAPHRAGM

When you exhale, your diaphragm moves back up and **relaxes.**

It's the work of your diaphragm! When you inhale, this rounded muscle contracts and moves down. Other muscles also pull your rib cage up and out at the same time. All this movement makes the space in your chest area bigger.

21

Quickly drinking water, holding your breath, and having someone scare you are all common ways people try to cure hiccups. If your hiccups last more than 2 days, it might be time to call a doctor.

FUN FACT: 16

SCIENTISTS AREN'T SURE WHY WE GET HICCUPS.

Hiccups happen when the muscles you use to breathe contract over and over on their own. This can happen if you swallow air by eating too fast or chewing gum. Hiccups can also be caused by more serious health problems.

YOUR RIBS HAVE MUSCLES THAT HELP YOU BREATHE!

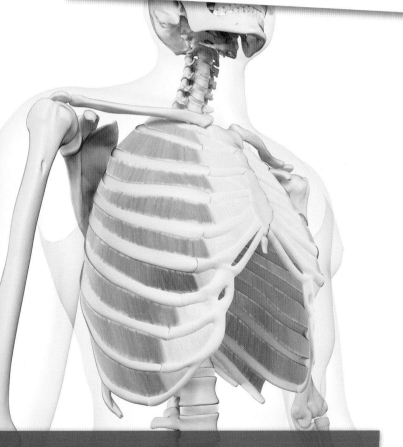

The muscles between your ribs are called the intercostal muscles.

The rib bones protect the lungs—but they need to be able to move. The rib muscles are found between the bones. They make the rib cage able to expand, or get bigger, when you inhale to give your lungs more room.

23

BREATH POWER

SCIENTISTS DON'T KNOW WHY PEOPLE YAWN.

One theory, or idea, is that the body might need more oxygen because you don't breathe as deeply as normal when you're tired. A big yawn brings in lots of oxygen, which causes carbon dioxide levels to go down.

Some scientists think yawns help people cool down their brains! Others think yawning might keep the lungs working properly by stretching them out or moving around an oily matter called surfactant.

Deep breathing can help slow down your heart and relax your muscles. This can help you feel less upset.

YOU CAN CONTROL SOME OF YOUR FEELINGS BY BREATHING.

Certain exercises have been shown to calm people down when they're upset. Breathing in for four counts and then out for four counts can help you **focus** better and calm down.

THE LONGEST ANYONE HAS EVER HELD THEIR BREATH WAS 24 MINUTES AND 3.45 SECONDS.

Don't try this at home! Most people can only hold their breath for a minute or two at a time. With careful practice and training, some people can learn to hold their breath for much longer.

Free divers don't bring oxygen on their dives. Some dive deeper than 800 feet (244 m) and hold their breath the whole time!

THE RESPIRATORY SYSTEM

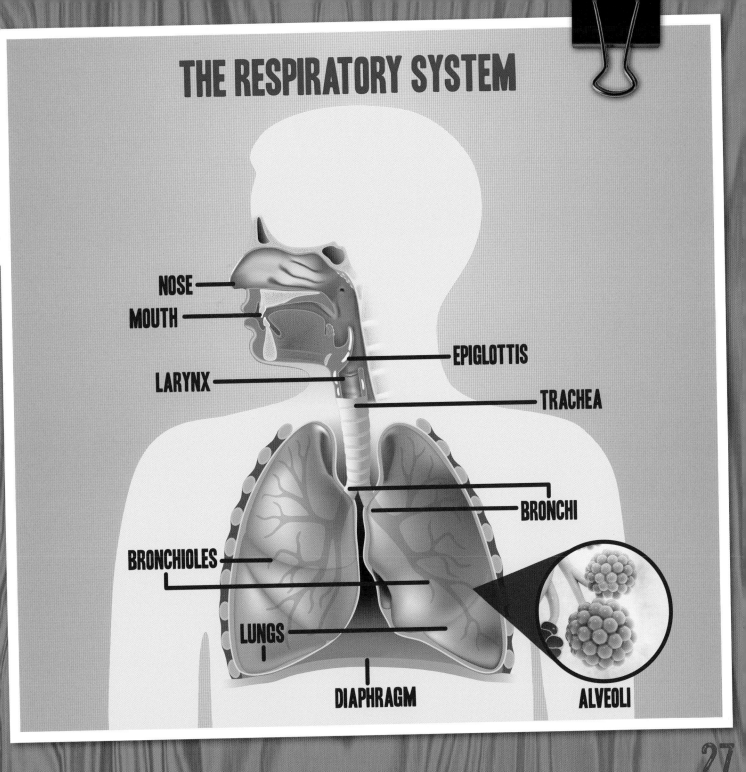

NOSE

MOUTH

LARYNX

EPIGLOTTIS

TRACHEA

BRONCHI

BRONCHIOLES

LUNGS

DIAPHRAGM

ALVEOLI

JUST BREATHE

Breathing is one of the most important things your body does, and you do it mostly without thinking. The respiratory system takes care of all the steps in the breathing process without requiring any brainpower. Most people are better at breathing than at almost anything else, and they don't even have to try!

Breathing keeps your blood healthy and your brain working. It helps your muscles work, allows you to talk, and protects you from dust, pollen, and germs. So take a deep breath!

Inhale for 4 seconds,
then exhale for 4 seconds.
Notice a difference?

GLOSSARY

filter: to collect bits from a liquid passing through

focus: to direct your attention or effort at something specific

humid: containing moisture

marathon: a running race that is 26.2 miles (42.1 km) long

mucus: a thick liquid produced in some parts of the body such as the nose and throat

muscle: one of the parts of the body that allow movement

organ: a part of the body (such as the heart or liver) that has a certain job

particle: a very small piece of something

protect: to keep safe

relax: to become less tense, tight, or stiff

surface area: the amount of area covered by the surface of something

vessel: a small tube that carries fluids to different parts of a person or animal's body

BOOKS

Brett, Flora. *Your Respiratory System Works!* North Mankato, MN: Capstone Press, 2015.

Gray, Susan H. *The Respiratory System.* Mankato, MN: Child's World, 2014.

WEBSITES

Lungs and Breathing

www.dkfindout.com/us/human-body/lungs-and-breathing/

Find out more about the respiratory system and other body systems here.

Your Lungs & Respiratory System

kidshealth.org/en/kids/lungs.html

Learn about the respiratory system by looking at diagrams, taking quizzes, and doing fun activities.

Publisher's note to educators and parents: Our editors have carefully reviewed these websites to ensure that they are suitable for students. Many websites change frequently, however, and we cannot guarantee that a site's future contents will continue to meet our high standards of quality and educational value. Be advised that students should be closely supervised whenever they access the internet.

INDEX